The Story of

Saint Patrick

Young Patrick heard shouting and noise in the middle of the night. He thought he was dreaming, but when he saw his father running into the room, he knew it was no dream.

“Patrick get up!” his father shouted. “We are being attacked and you must escape!”

Even though he tried to run away, 14-year-old Patrick was taken by the invaders. Soon he was bound in chains with other young men. It was the year 399 A.D., and sadly, these types of raids were very common.

Soon, Patrick found himself in the lower hold of a large ship making its way from his home in Scotland to Ireland. It was a frightening trip for a young boy. He thought of his parents and his home and wondered if he would ever see them again.

When they got to Ireland, Patrick was led off the ship. He was surprised by the many shades of green spread across the countryside. But he had little time to enjoy the view. Soon, he was lined up with other men and sold as a slave to a farmer.

The new country was a strange place for a Christian like Patrick. The people did not know about Christ and were very fearful and superstitious. Patrick had never seen anything like it, and it made him long for home even more.

His master forced him to herd the sheep. He spent long hours in the countryside doing his job as best he could in order to avoid punishment. It was a hard life for him. With no friends or anyone to talk with, Patrick began talking with God. He told God about everything that was happening to him. When he was sad, he would tell God about it. When the beautiful countryside brought him joy, he told God about that, too. The more Patrick prayed, the closer he felt to God.

As a result of his many prayers, Patrick learned that God cared about him. He thought of the other men he worked with and did his best to share his faith with them. Sadly, not many of them liked what they heard, and they made fun of Patrick.

Many years passed. Then one night, when Patrick was 20 years old, he had a strange dream. In the dream, Patrick saw a man pointing to a boat on the shore. "Your ship home is waiting for you!" the man in the dream said.

Patrick woke up right away. He thought to himself, *Could God be speaking to me?* A few nights later, Patrick quietly picked up his few belongings, tiptoed out from the camp, and then ran in the direction of the shore. He had escaped.

Tired from days of travel by foot, Patrick wearily made his ways through the hills until he reached the shore. Soon his heart was racing. There, right in front of him, was the boat from his dream. The men were about to set sail, but to his dismay, they would not let Patrick on board. So he did what he had learned to do: he prayed and told God his troubles. To Patrick's surprise, the men changed their minds. He was finally going home!

What a wonderful day it was when Patrick climbed the hill to his parent's house.

"This is a miracle!" his mother cried. "We thought we would never see you again!"

Soon Patrick was enjoying all the comforts of home. He had his own room, clean clothes, and loving family and friends. He quickly forgot his life as a slave, but he did not forget God. He thanked God for having freed him and for the many blessings he could now enjoy.

One night as Patrick slept soundly, he had another dream. In the dream, there were people calling out to him. "Holy man," the strangers begged. "Come back! Please come back to Ireland and help us!"

Patrick woke up. He wondered to himself, *Is God asking me to return to Ireland, the country where I was a slave?*

Patrick prayed about the dream. He could not forget the voices of the people in the dream calling out to him. Soon, he felt that God was indeed asking him to go back, but not as a slave. God was calling him to go back as a consecrated man of God. Patrick knew God was calling him to become a priest!

Patrick left home to study. He was a dedicated student, and in a few years he became a well-loved priest. As his faith grew, so did his faithfulness to the Church and her people. Later, he was made a Bishop. It was then that Patrick decided to return to Ireland.

It was a big step for Patrick. He returned to the very land from which he had escaped slavery. The people were surprised to see him, but they did not try to make him a slave. Instead, many listened to him. However, others did not like what Patrick had to say and sometimes chased him away.

So what did Patrick do? He prayed, and God answered, and began to do miracles through Patrick. In fact, God did so many miracles, that the Irish people started to take notice.

Many people began to accept Patrick's faith and to believe in and follow Jesus. Soon, Patrick began to set up churches throughout Ireland! The old religions of fear were soon driven away by the truth of the Christian faith!

Saint Patrick was a very courageous man. He got his courage through prayer. Prayer was the way in which Patrick came to know God. We can know God too, by spending time with Him, talking to Him in prayer, and receiving the grace that He loves to give us through His Son, Jesus. Let's always remember Patrick and share his story on Saint Patrick's Day!